GENERAL SERIES 104

The Poor Law in Nineteenth-Century England and Wales

ANNE DIGBY

The Historical Association

59a Kennington Park Road, London SE11 4JH

ACKNOWLEDGEMENTS

The cartoon on the outside front cover is *The "Milk" of the Poor-Law "Kindness"*, reproduced by the kind permission of *Punch*, published originally in 1843. It depicts the workhouse classification scheme of the New Poor Law in action: a mother in the workhouse at Bethnal Green separated from her five weeks old baby. The drawing on the outside back cover is of the Oxford Workhouse, built 1863-4, to a design by W. Fisher in a free Renaissance style, and later known as the Cowley Road Hospital; it was published originally in *The Builder*, 4 February 1865. The Dietaries reproduced on page 4 were used at Heckingham House, in the Loddon and Clavering Incorporation (later Union) in Norfolk under the Old, and New, Poor Laws. The former gave 250 ounces, the latter 178 ounces of solid food each week to an adult male pauper. They were published originally in F.M. Eden, *The State of the Poor* (1797) and *Second Report of the Poor Law Commissioners*, (pp. 1836, XXIX, part I). The graphs reproduced on pages 10, 24 and 25 were drawn by the author.

The publication of a pamphlet by the Historical Association does not necessarily imply the Association's official approbation of the opinions expressed therein.

©Anne Digby, 1982
ISBN 0 85278 250 0
H.A. 9.0682

Printed in Great Britain by
The Chameleon Press Limited,
5–25 Burr Road, London SW18 4SG.

Contents

Bill of Fare in the House of Industry.

	Breakfast.	Dinner.	Supper.
Sunday,	Bread and cheese, and butter, or treacle.	Dumplins, butcher's meat, and bread.	Bread and cheese, or butter.
Monday,	The same as Sunday.	Broth and bread.	Ditto.
Tuesday,	Milk and water gruel, and bread.	Baked suet puddings.	Ditto.
Wednesday,	The same as Sunday.	Dumplins and milk broth; or milk and water gruel.	Ditto.
Thursday,	The same as Tuesday.	The same as Sunday.	Ditto.
Friday,	The same as Sunday.	The same as Monday.	Ditto.
Saturday,	The same as Tuesday.	Bread and cheese, or butter.	Ditto.

The men are, each, allowed a pint of beer at every meal, except when they have broth, or gruel. Women, with children at the breast, have the same allowance. Others have two-thirds of a pint.

GENERAL DIETARY for the ABLE-BODIED.

		BREAKFAST.			DINNER.				SUPPER.		
		Bread.	Cheese.	Butter.	Meat Pudding, with Vegetables*.	Suet Pudding, with Vegetables*.	Bread.	Cheese.	Bread.	Cheese.	Butter.
		oz.	oz.	oz.	oz.	oz.	oz.	oz.	oz.	oz.	oz.
Sunday -	Men -	6	1	-	16	-	-	-	6	1	—
	Women	5	-	½	10	-	-	-	5	-	½
Monday -	Men -	6	1	-	-	-	7	1	6	1	—
	Women	5	-	½	-	-	7	1	5	-	½
Tuesday -	Men -	6	1	-	-	16	-	-	6	1	—
	Women	5	-	½	-	10	-	-	5	-	½
Wednesday,	Men -	6	1	-	-	-	7	1	6	1	—
	Women	5	-	½	-	-	7	1	5	-	½
Thursday	Men -	6	1	-	-	-	7	1	6	1	—
	Women	5	-	½	-	-	7	1	5	-	½
Friday -	Men -	6	1	-	-	16	-	-	6	1	—
	Women	5	-	½	-	10	-	-	5	-	½
Saturday	Men -	6	1	-	-	-	7	1	6	1	—
	Women	5	-	½	-	-	7	1	5	-	½

Old people, being all 60 years of age and upwards: the weekly addition of one ounce of tea, and milk or sugar; also an additional meat pudding dinner on Thursday in each week, in lieu of bread and cheese, to those for whose age and infirmities it may be deemed requisite.

Children under nine years of age: bread and milk for their breakfast and supper, or gruel when milk cannot be obtained; also such proportions of the dinner diet as may be requisite for their respective ages.

Sick: whatever is ordered for them by the medical officer.

* The vegetables are extra, and not included in the weight specified.

The Last Years of the Old Poor Law, 1790-1834

Variety rather than uniformity characterised the administration of poor relief in England and Wales, and at no period was this more apparent than in the decades before the national reform of the poor law in 1834. Unprecedented economic and social changes produced severe problems for those responsible for social welfare, and different localities found distinctive solutions to them within the broad legal framework laid down by the Elizabethan Poor Law of 1597-1601. A social policy designed for a predominantly rural population of some four million people was likely to need some adaptation to meet the needs of a more urbanised population which increased dramatically in size from six to nine millions during the second half of the eighteenth century, and from nine to fourteen millions by 1834. The problems posed for relief administrators were least in the fast-growing towns of northern England where the expansion of iron or textile industries provided work for the growing numbers of inhabitants, and greatest for those in the countryside of southern England where economic changes exacerbated demographic pressures. During the Revolutionary and Napoleonic Wars, higher food prices encouraged farmers to raise production by enclosing land, and 2000 acts of enclosure were passed at this time. While enclosure increased the amount of employment available, it did not do so sufficiently to absorb all those in the expanded rural population. Also, the accompanying loss of common rights (such as the right to graze a cow or collect wood for fuel) caused some hardship to the poor. These difficulties were increased by the decline of cottage industries, particularly hand-spinning and weaving, which could not compete with the new factory-based production. Worse was to follow after the end of the wars, when a slump in the average price of wheat led to agrarian depression, with a consequent reduction in farm employment and a rise in the number of able-bodied applicants for poor relief. It was in southern England, where the rural labourer had little alternative to agricultural employment, that the dimensions of the poverty problem were most obvious.

These social and economic changes underlined the growing significance of the able-bodied among those relieved by poor-law administrators. The Elizabethan, or Old, Poor Law had divided the poverty-stricken into three categories: the 'able-bodied' poor who could not find employment and who were to have work provided for them; the rogues, vagabonds, and sturdy beggars who were to be whipped or otherwise punished for their disinclination to work; and the 'impotent' poor (the old, sick, or handicapped), who were to be relieved in almshouses. This complex administrative task was entrusted to some fifteen thousand parishes, each of which appointed overseers as administrators and levied a poor rate to finance relief. Later, it was found necessary to restrict the numbers of poor people for whom local ratepayers were responsible, and in 1662 an Act for the Better Relief of the Poor gave overseers power to remove anybody who was likely to become chargeable and who did not possess a settlement guaranteeing the right to relief in the parish. In 1723 Knatchbull's General Workhouse Act was passed which enabled single parishes to erect a workhouse, if they wished, so that they could enforce labour on the able-bodied poor in return for relief. By 1776, when the first official returns were made, there were almost 2000 of them in England; typically each held only 20 to 50 inmates. But by this time the high costs of indoor relief, and attendant problems of inefficient workhouse management, were reinforcing social pressures for a more sympathetic treatment of the poor. As a result Gilbert's Act of 1782 allowed parishes to combine into unions where the unemployed able-bodied poor were provided first with outdoor relief and then with employment, while indoor relief in poorhouses was confined to caring for the old, sick, infirm and their dependent children.

This revival of interest in outdoor relief for the able-bodied poor coincided with much greater under-employment in rural areas from the 1780s. Systematic scales of outdoor allowances appear to have been associated with years when bad harvests and soaring food prices led to an acute fall in the real wages of those rural labourers who were in employment. Although the Speenhamland scale of May 1795 has given its name to these allowances, this was not because it was the first of its type, but because F.M. Eden made it the best-known example by publicising it in his classic account, *The State of the Poor* (1797). Earlier schemes to subsidise labourers' wages had appeared; in Cambridgeshire this occurred as early as 1785. The bread crises of the 1790s, in which poor harvests caused extremely high prices, stimulated local action to alleviate the sufferings of the poor, and as these bread crises recurred, so the tendency to systematise relief in formal scales increased. It would be incorrect to think that such scales were either permanently adhered to in the period that followed, or that they were practised universally. Indeed, it is misleading to view the years from 1795 to 1834 as the 'Speenhamland period' characterised by regular payments to the able-bodied poor based on scales. There were wide differences between and within counties. An increasing amount of evidence indicates that even a broad division of England into Speenhamland and non-Speenhamland counties is inaccurate and conceals an obstinate diversity of parochial practice. This variety is also indicated by the fact that while the general trend was to adopt allowances in the 1820s, some sixty parishes are known to have abandoned them at this time.

In the agragrian depression after the end of the Napoleonic Wars the necessity to spread a limited amount of employment among an increasing population produced not only allowances but also an increasing number of make-work schemes. Some parishes used the roundsmen system, by which paupers were sent round to work for the farmers of the parishes in turn, and their wages were supplemented from the parish poor rate. Other parishes set up a more formal system known as the labour rate, in which a separate rate was levied on occupiers, and employers could choose either to pay their share of the rate or use their contribution to employ labourers (with settlements in the parish) at the going wage-rate. None of these expedients did much to alleviate underlying economic problems. In rural areas the ratepayers who financed poor-law employment schemes were usually the same body of farmers who felt themselves to be too impoverished to offer adequate work and remuneration to the labourer. In consequence, the practice of subsidising wages by poor relief tended to drive down wages still further. An alternative scheme, by which the parish directly employed paupers on the roads and paid them from the highway rate, still meant that it was the same parishioners who financed relief, and the effect on local employment patterns was therefore similar. This increasing complexity of poor-law administration was associated in some parishes with more professional administration by paid assistant overseers, and in others by small parish committees called select vestries. Lancashire and Yorkshire were particularly zealous in forming select vestries, and tended in consequence to think that the 1834 Act was irrelevant to the North.

In the closing decades of the Old Poor Law, local administrators directed their efforts primarily at the outdoor poor. They continued to administer a large number of poor-law institutions but the substantial increase (of perhaps one-fifth) in the number of such institutions between 1776 and 1803 was not continued; there was only a slight increase in the next decade and little evidence of growth thereafter. This may have been because the costs of indoor relief were four times higher than those of outdoor relief, as the official returns of 1803 indicated. Some parishes tried to reduce the costs of relief in the workhouse by 'farming their poor', paying an entrepreneur a fixed sum per week for each pauper inmate and allowing him to make what profit he could by depressing the costs of maintenance, but the number of parishes which did this was smaller than was once thought. Whilst it is true that in some workhouses the paupers suffered from cruelty and neglect, in others the material standard of living appears to have been quite generous, as can be seen from surviving dietaries. Smaller workhouses found it impossible to provide specialist facilities for their different categories of inmates, but the larger houses of industry were capable of organising quite humane facilities for the aged, the sick, and the children. A growth in the provision of social welfare during the closing years of the Old Poor Law meant that some parishes and unions approximated to a welfare state in miniature. Many of the deserving poor – the old, sick, young children, and one-parent families – had the security of regular payments from the parochial pension-list. Housing was obtained for some of them, either through rent paid by the overseers, or by the provision of 'parish' or 'town' houses. Overseers' accounts recorded the payment not only of cash but of clothes and fuel. Some attempt was made, albeit with little success, to see that pauper children might later earn a livelihood, either through teaching them a trade in the workhouse or through apprenticeships outside it. Parochial medical services, though provided on a less comprehensive basis than those instituted later under the New Poor Law, were more efficient under the Old Poor Law than was once thought. Many parishes appointed a doctor to visit the poor in their own homes.

Towards Reform

The range of social benefits conferred by the Old Poor Law may impress the historian but its cost alarmed contemporaries. Much of the dissatisfaction which triggered reform in 1834 focussed on what were considered to be unacceptably burdensome poor rates. The *Report* issued by the Royal Commission on the Poor Laws in 1834 criticised the rating system as being 'in the highest degree uncertain and capricious' and condemned the unfair use of old rating valuations and of rating exemptions.

How far does available evidence support contemporary opinion that the rating system was oppressive? The agricultural community had a grievance in that the narrow Elizabethan base of the poor law, which rated land and buildings but not personal or moveable wealth, benefited the industrial and commercial classes at its expense. This inequity grew as poor rates increased rapidly in the early nineteenth century. Poor rates for England and Wales had amounted to £5.3 millions in 1802-3, rose to £8.6 millions by 1813, reached an unprecedented figure of £9.3 millions by 1817-18, and after lower levels in the 1820s, rose again to reach a second peak of £8.6 millions in 1831-2 and 1832-3, (see figure 1). There was thus a rise in poor rates of 62% from 1802-3 to 1832-3. Meanwhile the value of gross rentals of farm land, which were related to many assessments for the poor rate, did not increase to the same extent. There was a rise of only 25% in the same period, from £28 millions in 1800 to £35 millions in 1830. Whether landlord or farmer was hardest hit is uncertain. Occupiers (tenant farmers) were formally responsible for paying rates, but may in practice have been able to transfer all or part of the burden to landowners by negotiating lower rentals. Attempts by farmers to make such transfers certainly contributed to worsening relationships in rural society. Meanwhile it is important to remember that population in England and Wales increased from nine to fourteen millions, which meant that relief expenditure per head did not rise as much as the totals for poor rates or relief expenditure. *Per capita* relief expenditures in the early 1830s were 9 or 10 shillings per head of the population compared with 12 or 13 shillings in 1816 to 1819.

In the years preceding the introduction of the New Poor Law, opinion was hardening against the poor. E.P. Thompson has drawn

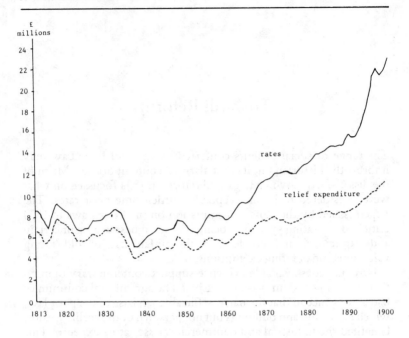

Figure 1: Poor Rates and Relief Expenditure in England and Wales, 1813-1900. Sources: Poor Rate Returns and Annual Reports of Poor Law Commission, Poor Law Board and Local Government Board

attention to the displacement of 'moral economy' by political economy. The traditional rights of the poor were being eroded, and a humane relationship between men of different status and income was often replaced by a narrower cash nexus. This was evident not only in independent employment but also in the administration of the poor law. For example, the Cambridgeshire country bread scale of 1821 provided for only two-thirds of the relief in terms of bread price that had been allowed for in the scale adopted in parts of the country in 1783. Stringent relief scales, low wages, and large-scale under-employment created such depths of misery for the agricultural labourer of southern England that desperation erupted in the widespread 'Swing' riots of 1830-1. This produced immediate wage concessions by employers and more generous relief from parish overseers, but both wages and allowances tended to be scaled down thereafter and were thus only temporary gains for the poor. A more permanent result was an increasingly punitive attitude to the poor: it was thought that since a paternalistic system of relief had failed to cement their loyalty, a harsher system of social control might ensure their subordination. It seems likely that the riots dealt a mortal blow to the Old Poor Law and accelerated reform.

The desirability of reform had been debated since the late eighteenth century. In the early stages of this intermittent discussion evangelicals and humanitarians were prominent in urging that the poor should be treated liberally, but the opposing views of political economists were increasingly insistent. They argued that a statutory poor law was undesirable because it distorted the free market mechanism for determining natural levels of prices and wages. Among them was T.R. Malthus, who believed that the existing system of poor relief, by encouraging early marriages and large families, created the very poor it was designed to relieve; and hence should be abolished. The sheer impracticability of total abolition meant that much discussion was along reformist lines, but it is likely that the abolitionist case made more stringent reforms acceptable to public opinion. Contemporaries were as much concerned by the moral, as the economic, effects of pauperism. The Select Committee on Labourer's Wages of 1824 stated that 'by far the worst consequence of the system is the degradation of the character of the labouring class'. Six years later, the Swing riots of 1830-1 must have appeared to give substance to that view for many of the propertied classes. Shortly afterwards, in February 1832, a Whig ministry appointed a Royal Commission to investigate the operation of the poor laws.

In the autumn of 1832 the commission appointed 26 assistants to visit the localities, and to report back on questions covering the form of relief and on the administrators, paupers, and ratepayers. Not only did the assistants write up their conclusions at length, after visiting one-fifth of the parishes, but also the *Town Queries* and *Rural Queries* which they sent out in August 1832 elicited replies from one-tenth of the parishes, containing one-fifth of the population. The Commission's apparent enthusiasm for empirical research concealed firm preconceptions about the desirable nature of reform, and the 'facts' they discovered were utilised selectively to support them. It is revealing that their assistants' reports and the replies of the parishes, which should have provided substantive evidence for their reforms, were not published until much later.

The *Report* published by the Commission in February 1834 condemned a system which relieved mere poverty (rather than absolute destitution) as both economically and morally disastrous, and concluded that 'the great source of abuse is outdoor relief afforded to the able-bodied'. Modern historians have blamed the two authors of the *Report*, Edwin Chadwick and Nassau Senior, for a blinkered approach which caused them to select evidence in favour of their own view. Mark Blaug views their *Report* as 'not only a "wildly unhistorical document" as Tawney once said, but also a wildly unstatistical one' (Blaug, 1964, p. 243). He suggests that the replies to Rural and Town Queries were ignored when they challenged pre-determined conclusions. The evidence actually indicated that Speenhamland allowances were not universally practised and thus threw doubt on the Commission's allegation that there was a dynamic process of ever-increasing pauperism. Blaug's deduction from this contemporary evidence is that Speenhamland allowances were given up before 1832, and that the system castigated by the *Report* as being in urgent need of reform ironically was already in decline.

An alternative interpretation has been put forward by D.A. Baugh. His quantitative analysis of surviving parish accounts in Essex, Kent and Sussex, indicated that 'the Speenhamland system did not matter much at any time' (Baugh, 1975, p. 67). He argues that the changing shape of the poverty problem in the period from 1790 to 1834 dictated the pattern of relief. Before 1814 few bread scales were utilised, but the post-war agrarian depression induced more parishes than hitherto to adopt both bread scales and family allowances. Even at this time there was not the 'snow-balling' of *per capita* relief expenditures which might have been expected if the Royal Commission's analyses had been accurate. Recent analysis by D. McCloskey has indicated that the *Report's* view of allowances as both decreasing labour supplied, and lowering wages is theoretically untenable given a constant demand for labour. Instead, allowances, in the form either of children's allowances, or payment in aid of wages, should be regarded as an income subsidy. Here, the relief given in response to need guaranteed a minimum income and thus reduced the amount of work the labourer supplied. Only in the case of less widespread practices - the roundsmen and labour rate systems - did the Old Poor Law act to some extent as a wage subsidy. It was in this context only that the labour supply increased and independent wages fell. This argument supports Blaug's assertion that structural unemployment was the real problem in the countryside. It was the surplus labour problem which fostered the allowance system and not, as the *Report* alleged, the proliferation of relief which pauperised the labourer. Complementing this economic analysis, there has been a demographic study of the relationship between allowances and population increase. The Royal Commission on the Poor Laws of 1832-4 followed Malthus in reasoning that generous allowances led to early marriages and larger families. But an interesting study by J.P. Huzel has turned this hypothesis on its head and concluded, 'Just as Blaug has argued that the allowance system was more a reaction to low wages than a cause, so it might be suggested that this system was a response rather than a stimulus to population increase' (Huzel, 1930, p. 378).

Recent investigations on the Old Poor Law by historians, economists, and demographers have therefore produced convergent conclusions. They emphasise that relief under the Old Poor Law was essentially a response to population growth, under-employment, and low wages, rather than their cause as the Royal Commission's *Report* alleged. Unfortunately the *Report's* incorrect diagnoses underlay the policies adopted in the Poor Law Amendment Act, and thus limited its effectiveness.

The Poor Law Amendment Act of 1834 and its Administrative Implementation

The Poor Law Amendment Act has been seen as the major watershed in the nineteenth-century poor law, dividing the the parochial variety of the Old Poor Law from the centralised uniformity of the New. It has been represented as a notably powerful intervention by the state in the affairs of localities: an example of Benthamite orthodoxy, imposing uniformity upon poor-law practice. At the same time the 1834 act has been interpreted as a major divide in social values, symbolising a change from paternalism to the pursuit of class interests in the administration of social welfare. A complementary view has been that the Act represented a triumph for classical economics, liberating the labour market from distortions imposed by the Old Poor Law and thereby benefiting capitalism. In the following analysis we shall see to what extent the available evidence substantiates these hypotheses.

The Act

The bill for the reform of the poor law, introduced in April 1834, commanded sufficient support in Parliament to pass swiftly into law by August of the same year. Its provisions reflected the concerns of the Royal Commission in aiming at the economic and moral independence of the able-bodied labourer. Under the new system it was not sufficient merely to be poor to qualify for relief: the able-bodied actually had to be destitute, and the mechanism for distinguishing between these two states was to be the workhouse. This institution was to be the only method of relieving the adult able-bodied, and its conditions were to be deterrent ones, in that they were to be 'less eligible', or less attractive, than those enjoyed by the independent labourer. The workhouse would thus be a self-operating test, for only the truly indigent would wish to enter such an institution. In order to generate sufficient finance to build workhouses, parishes were to be grouped into poor law unions. Each union was to be administered by professional, salaried officers who were to work under boards of elected guardians of the poor. But local autonomy was to be curtailed in the interests of uniformity: local boards were to be supervised by a newly created central body - the Poor Law Commission and its inspectorate.

The 1834 act appears most obviously as an interventionist and collectivist measure, but it would be shortsighted to ignore elements in it which contradicted this apparent increase in the powers of central government, and which in fact strengthened local government. This tension within the legislation reflected the opposing influences which shaped it. Benthamite opinion, shared by the authors of the *Report*, favoured centralization to achieve uniformity and efficiency but ran counter to the vested interests in local autonomy possessed by a powerful, landed interest in Parliament. David Roberts has concluded that the central poor-law body came to possess an unprecedentedly 'vast accumulation of powers, legislative, judicial and administrative', but that local government, far from being supplanted, was actually strengthened by the formation of the new local unions (Roberts, 1960, p. 109). For many years local and central authorities coexisted uneasily in the administration of the New Poor Law, but the novel 'professional bureaucratic values' of the latter were eventually to mould the objectives and methods of local guardians of the poor (Lubenow, 1971, p. 40). Local autonomy was not so much overthrown by frontal assaults, in the form of policy directives from a central authority, as insidiously submerged under expert advice and bureaucratic red tape. By the end of the century 'the poor law mind' was as much a feature of administrative attitudes in the localities as it was of those at the centre.

The Administrative Implementation of the Act

The continuing power of local property owners was shown in the creation of poor-law unions. The newly-created central board, known as the Poor Law Commission, sent an assistant poor-law commissioner to form poor-law unions in each county. He did this by calling a meeting in the existing govermental areas of the hundred or the borough, at which landowners, magistrates, and men of substance were well-represented and gave their views on desirable union boundaries. In many areas boundaries were also shaped by the continued existence of Gilbert Unions and incorporations under local act. As the commissioners worked from the south to the north of England, they found themselves having to form unions much more hastily if they were to be ready in time to serve as units for the Registration Act of 1837, which began civil registration of births, marriages and deaths. As a result of these pressures, the Poor Law Commissioners' original model – in which unions of equal size should be centred on a market town – was frequently disregarded. Nevertheless 15,000 parishes were amalgamated into some 600 unions to achieve the poor-law geography of the 1834 act.

Lord John Russell, the leader of the Whig ministry which passed the Poor Law Amendment Act, said in 1847 that its 'real object ... was to establish self-government in the localities' (Brundage, 1978, p. 159). The nature of this self-government depended on the social composition of the new boards of guardians. In the early years, the gentry and aristocracy played a prominent role on many boards, not because they were elected on to them but because they served as *ex officio* members by virtue of their position as magistrates. But once important decisions had been made over union boundaries, the site and cost of workhouses, and the appointment of officials, many *ex officio* members found routine business too tedious to to merit their weekly, or fortnightly, attendance at the board. The elected guardians were then able to assert themselves: in rural areas these were predominantly farmers, and in urban areas, tradesmen. Nassau Senior, one of the authors of the Royal Commission's *Report,* commented that 'the guardians elected by owners and rate-payers are succeeding to the influence of the magistrates ... All sorts of local ambitions are everywhere at work' (Lubenow, 1971, p. 29). These local ambitions had a strong political dimension, since the power wielded by boards of guardians made them intrinsically political bodies. The workhouse was often an issue in both local and national elections, and Tories sought electoral advantage in depicting their opponents as 'Workhouse Whigs' (Fraser, 1976).

The decision to build a workhouse was a local one needing the consent of a majority on the board of guardians. The central poor law board could order the alteration or enlargement of an existing workhouse but had no authority to compel a new one to be erected. Effectively, therefore, the ability of the central board to force an implementation of the 1834 act, with its crucial mechanism of a workhouse test, was extremely weak. Instead, it had to rely on the persuasive tactics of its agents in the field - the assistant commissioners or inspectors. These must be accounted a success in that within five years of the Poor Law Amendment Act some 350 workhouses had been built. Nearly all were situated in the rural south of England. Many of them had been influenced by the four model workhouse designs published by the Poor Law Commissioners in 1835. These specified a single union building (rather than specialist accommodation), and thus ushered in the general mixed workhouse.

The workhouses obviously provided a better standard of physical accommodation than that found in labourers' cottages. Was this superior eligibility also reflected in paupers' diets? Or was Dickens, in *Oliver Twist,* accurate in describing poor people as having the alternative 'of being starved by a gradual process in the house, or by a quick one out of it'? Apparently not, if one looks at the Poor Law Commission's six model dietaries from which local guardians selected one which approximated to the diet of labourers in their area. The dietaries contained 160-70 ounces of solid food per week for adult inmates, or about one-third more than an agricultural labourer in the rural south would obtain. Much of the diet consisted of cheap carbohydrates - bread, potatoes, suet pudding – but there was provision for a meat meal once, twice, or three times a week, and additional protein was provided through cheese at breakfast or supper. Unappealing the workhouse dietary may have been, but in spite of the rumours that circulated during the first years of the New Poor Law it is clear that paupers did not starve within the workhouse.

The cruelty of the workhouse did not reside in its material deprivation but in its psychological harshness. Indeed, the Poor Law Commissioners themselves appreciated that it was through psychological rather than material deterrence that the workhouse test would operate. A potent means for achieving this, as in so many institutions, was through depersonalising the individual. An obvious device was the issue of pauper uniforms, sometimes stamped prominently with the name of the union. Thus attired, the inmate lived a monotonous and regimented existence. The workhouse rules laid down that the adult inmate should rise at 5 a.m. in the summer (and 7 a.m. in winter), should be set to work from 7 a.m. (or 8 a.m. in winter) to 12 noon, and from 1 p.m. to 6 p.m., and should go to bed at 8 p.m. The Master of the Workhouse was instructed to 'enforce industry, order, punctuality and cleanliness' on the inmates. Except in large, efficiently-conducted workhouses the labour extracted from the indoor pauper was not as onerous as the rules suggested. Able-bodied women were likely to experience hard labour in a laundry, and other domestic work, but male inmates were prone to suffer the tedium of under-employment.

The main element of psychological deterrence in the union workhouse was its system of classifying inmates. Labourers in Cambridgeshire stated in a petition to Parliament in 1836 that they were 'dismayed and disgusted beyond anything they can describe, with the idea of being shut up in one part of a prison and their wives and children in other separate parts because they are poor through no fault of their own' (WEA, 1978). Such feelings must have been a common reaction to the seven-fold workhouse classifications under which inmates were divided into aged or infirm men or women, able-bodied men or women over 16 years of age, boys or girls aged from 7 to 15 years, and children under 7 years of age. Each category was assigned to its own day rooms, sleeping rooms, and exercise yards in the workhouse. Members of families who were separated in this unfeeling way might see each other, but not speak, during communal meals or at chapel. They were permitted to meet together only at infrequent intervals, and at the discretion of the guardians. In addition, young children were usually permitted to sleep with their mother at night, and to be with her during her leisure daytime hours.

The imposition of the administrative framework of the New Poor Law was therefore reasonably successful: unions were created even if these were of disparate size and composition; many workhouses were either built or enlarged; and less eligibility for paupers within them was achieved through psychological rather than material means. The central board was to encounter far more problems in attempts to force localities to adopt reformed relief policies.

The Persistence of the Allowance
System after 1834

'At best it is a most unthankful duty to fill a parochial office' wrote John Player, the overseer of the Essex town of Saffron Walden, in 1831, and his opinion remained unchanged when, after the enactment of the New Poor Law, he became one of the town's guardians. The onerous and unpopular nature of poor-law administration must have encouraged a self-interested approach to their duties amongst all but the noblest natures on boards of guardians. It is hardly surprising that nepotism operated in the appointment of salaried officers, and that allocations of contracts for supplies to workhouses was inefficient and sometimes corrupt. By the 1840s it became apparent that central supervision of local boards was ineffectual, since it was limited to a twice-yearly visit by an overworked poor-law inspector and to the regular submission of returns of paupers and of expenditure to the Poor Law Commission. This left substantial room for manoeuvre in the localities. It encouraged the development by boards of guardians of relief policies which owed less to the provisions of the 1834 act than to the convenience of administrators and the pockets of local ratepayers. Very limited progress was made by the central board in the North of England, in London, and in rural unions.

In the North, opposition to the New Poor Law was broad-based, involving both popular resistance and hostility from some propertied groups. The Anti-Poor Law movement of 1837-8 was centred on the textile towns of the West Riding of Yorkshire and Lancashire. It was a logical extension of the Ten Hours Movement, and was often organized by short-time committees which had been running the campaign for factory reform. This proved useful in welding together conservatives (who defended the localities against centralist attempts to overthrow a system of poor relief which they regarded as already sufficiently well organized), and radicals (who defended poor men against the inhumanity of the 'bastiles'). There were some spectacular incidents: at Oldham, guardian's elections were successfully boycotted; at Huddersfield, refusal to elect a clerk checked the introduction of the new system; at Todmorden (home town of John Fielden, the chief spokesman of the Anti-Poor Law Movement in Parliament), riots by local ratepayers led to military intervention. By the end of 1838, however, the steady progress of the Poor Law Commission in introducing the new system into some other northern counties made the more radical of the Anti-Poor Law leaders, like Feargus O'Connor, conclude that popular agitation had better be turned towards reforming the corrupt Parliament which had devised such an evil system. The movement thus became subsumed within Chartism.

The success of the Poor Law Commission in implementing the New Poor Law depended partly on the personality of the poor law inspectors who were the missionaries of the central board in this endeavour. The urbane Sir John Walsham had much greater success in the North-East than the more intemperate Charles Mott in Lancashire and the West Riding, where matters were also made worse by the rigid personality of Alfred Power, already disliked for his earlier work as a factory commissioner in 1833. The introduction of the new system also depended on the nature of the local economy: the mixed industrial economy of Durham and Northumberland was more stable than that of textile towns in Lancashire or the West Riding, and the futility of a workhouse system as a means of relieving large numbers of unemployed workers during a trade depression was therefore less glaringly obvious. In the North-East, the comparative prosperity of the region, together with the flexibility and commonsense of Walsham, contributed to a smooth and efficient imposition of the workhouse system. By 1841 every Durham union had a new or renovated workhouse. Both indoor and outdoor relief were at first administered relatively humanely and generously, and it was not until the downturn of trade and the arrival of the 'Hungry Forties', that the harsh impact of the New Poor Law was felt in County Durham. Increased numbers of those seeking relief and spiralling relief expenditures, led local boards to make stringent economies: a deterrent workhouse regime was adopted and a higher proportion of paupers – especially the able-bodied – was forced to accept relief there.

The substantial autonomy found among local guardians in Durham was also evident in predominantly urban unions in other northern counties. In Lancashire the forceful pressure of the Anti-Poor Law Movement had induced wariness in the members of the Poor Law Commission; they were conciliatory in requiring only a nominal submission to their orders. It was not until the 1850s and 1860s that new workhouses were built, so that the workhouse test was largely inoperative in the county during the mid-nineteenth century. Lancashire was thus relatively untouched by the 1834 act and until the 1860s poor-law administration there showed more signs of continuity than of change. In the West Riding of Yorkshire, even the geography of the new unions was not completed until the 1860s, while the workhouse system of the New Poor Law was only implemented on local initiative after 1847. It was adopted as a means of discouraging applications from the mobile poor: the English workers thrown out of work by industrial depression and, more pressingly, the large numbers of Irish pouring into the North of England after the Potato Famine of 1846.

This stubborn defence of local autonomy by many northern boards of guardians forced the Poor Law Commission, and its successor after 1847, the Poor Law Board, into making substantial concessions over the relief of the able-bodied poor. More amenable boards of guardians in the south had by 1841 been issued with orders prohibiting outdoor relief to the adult able-bodied poor. Nearly four-fifths of the unions received these orders. During the following year they were issued to rural unions in the north of England. In 1844 a general order consolidated these gains, and this Outdoor Relief Prohibitory Order was given to nearly all those areas previously issued with individual orders. Although this prohibitory order came closest of all the relief orders to the principles of 1834, it was evident that under its eight exceptions guardians might easily relieve the able-bodied poor on the grounds of 'sudden and urgent necessity', accident, or (alleged) sickness. Meanwhile, other unions had been issued in 1842 with a Labour Test Order, which laid down that where workhouse accommodation was inadequate to take in all who applied for relief, the needs of adult male able-bodied applicants should be tested by task work. By 1847 (when the Poor Law Commission's authority ended), a very complex situation had arisen in which 73.6% of unions were under the 1844 order, 11.3% under a labour test order, and 15% under both orders. In April 1852 the Poor Law Board attempted to bring large provincial towns, the metropolis, and northern industrial areas under more stringent regulation, but storms of protest led to an amended Outdoor Relief Regulation Order in the following December. This omitted the compulsion to prohibit relief to the adult able-bodied without a labour test, and also left out the instruction to pay part of such relief in kind - in the form of bread or flour. After 1852 the Poor Law Board retreated still further, reducing the number of unions operating the more stringent 1844 order from 396 to 307, and mitigating its force in a further 217 unions by issuing an alternative labour-test order. When the Poor Law Board was succeeded by the Local Government Board in 1871 only one in six unions were within the straitjacket of the 1844 order alone, and thus operating according to the 'principles of 1834'.

The allowance system therefore continued to operate in many areas during the mid-nineteenth century and flourished with particular vigour in the 'oases of independence' formed by unions or incorporations created before 1834 by local acts or by Gilbert's Act. However, a two-fold process reduced gradually the numbers of independent areas to negligible proportions: on the one hand, acts passed in 1843, 1847 and 1867 removed local exemptions; and on the other, local incorporations decided to end their autonomy and be assimilated into a national pattern. As a result the 1.5 million people who were outside the provisions of the 1834 Act in 1847 had shrunk to only 180,000 by the end of 1868. The most important extension of the power of the central board came with the Metropolitan Poor Act of 1867, which ended the substantial independence of many parts of London, and threatened to end their openly-acknowledged operation of the allowance system.

The central authority admitted to some extent the problems it encountered in attempting to impose the reformed system on the industrial North of England and on London. But the countryside of southern England, whose depths of pauperism had been highlighted by the Royal Commission of 1832-4, was the chief target for reform and allegedly the main success. Was this in fact the case? During the Commons debates on the Poor Law Amendment Bill in May 1834, a speaker warned against delivering the rural administration of the poor law into the hands of 'flinty-hearted and bargain-driving farmers – insolvent struggling men ... whose first and only object was to save their pence'. In the early years of the New Poor Law these economical instincts led to agreement on relief policies between the central poor-law authority and the farmers who formed the majority of elected members on local boards of guardians in country areas. The workhouse test promised substantial savings to hard-pressed rural ratepayers; and so, in rural, southern England poor-law inspectors found it relatively easy to form unions, to persuade local boards to erect workhouses, and to cut outdoor relief to the adult able-bodied to such a low level that it was possible for a prohibitory order to be issued to the union by 1840 or 1841. In this halcyon period the *Reports* of the Poor Law Commission and its inspectorate were self-congratulatory, emphasising that the end of allowances in aid of wages had produced an upright independence among labourers instead of a demoralised dependence, and that increased employment had ended the problem of surplus labour in the countryside.

These successes were in some cases more apparent than real: evidence selectively written up by 'copywriters' advertising the effectiveness of the New Poor Law. Edwin Chadwick, the disillusioned Secretary to the Poor Law Commission, revealed that the inspectors did not tell the central board of abuses in their districts because such reports were not well-received. Nevertheless, there were warning signals, even in the heavily edited version of events which appeared in the Poor Law Commission's annual *Reports*. In 1841 an inspector warned of the very wide discretionary powers available to the guardians in administering outdoor relief to the able-bodied. The following year the central board admitted that with a staff of only 10 inspectors their visits to localities would be infrequent. Following disclosures at Andover Workhouse (a notorious, if atypical, case), where hungry paupers had been reduced to gnawing putrid bones, a Select Committee in 1846 concluded that inspectors could not detect abuses because their districts were too large. The abuse that was either not detected, or – as Chadwick suggested – not publicised, was a revival of the allowance system in rural unions during the 1840s. There is a growing amount of evidence of widespread evasion of the prohibitory order in the rural unions of southern England after the onset of more difficult farming conditions in 1842.

In country unions in eastern and southern England and in the Midlands, outdoor allowances were frequently given to adult able-bodied labourers on the alleged ground of sickness. This exception to the prohibitory order was used by farmer–guardians from the 1840s to the 1890s to administer allowances in aid of wages. As the main class of rural ratepayers, the farmers on rural boards of guardians preferred outdoor relief because it cost only half as much as indoor relief. In addition, as employers, they found allowances convenient because they kept labourers close at hand rather than in a distant workhouse, and kept them in the locality during winter (when employment was slack) at less cost than if they had had to be paid wages. The farmer-guardians' power was exploited with singleminded selfishness except in rare cases where a powerful personality managed for a time to enforce the principles of 1834. This occurred most conspicuously in the Atcham Union in Shropshire under the guidance of Sir Baldwin Leighton.

The attempt to enforce the relief policies of the New Poor Law during the mid-nineteenth century was only partially successful. A reduction in relief expenditure of 28% from 1834 to 1840 indicated a more vigorous definition of need and a reduction in the amount of relief given (see figure 1) but it was not matched by a corresponding reduction in the incidence of outdoor allowances. In many northern areas political independence and a feeling that the workhouse system was irrelevant to the needs of an industrial economy delayed the impact of reform; and in numerous rural unions initial acquiescence was followed by a subversion of the relief regulations. The central poor law board was obliged to recognise the force of local resistance to an ending of the allowance system: by 1870 five out of six unions were under centrally-devised relief regulations which modified the 'principles of 1834'.

For those who continued to believe in the tenets of the Poor Law Amendment Act there was thus an urgent need to increase the proportion of indoor relief administered. The temporary collapse of the poor law in Lancashire and London, followed in 1870 by the

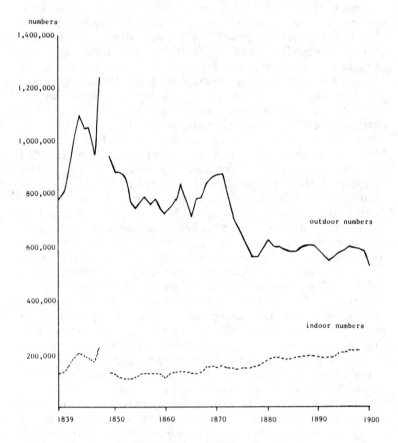

Figure 2: Numbers Relieved Inside and Outside the
Workhouse, 1839-1900; it should be noted that the figures
for 1839-47 are based on the quarter ending 25 March of
each year, and those for 1849-98 on the mean of figures
for 1 January and 1 July of each year. They are thus not
directly comparable. Sources: Reports of Poor Law
Commission, and T. MacKay,
A History of the English Poor Law *(1900), appendix.*

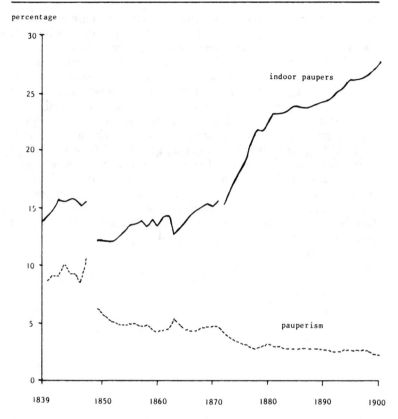

*Figure 3: Percentage of Pauperism on Population, and of
Paupers Relieved Inside the Workhouse, 1839-1900.
See figure 2 (page 24) for note and sources.*

revelation that the number of paupers exceeded one million, produced an alarmist reaction. In 1871 the newly-established Local Government Board dusted down the 'principles of 1834', and mounted an assault on allowances. (See figures 2 and 3.) Its crusading inspectors achieved considerable success in persuading local boards of guardians to reduce the amount of outdoor relief and especially that given to adult able-bodied males. Its work was facilitated in London by the Metropolitan Poor Law Amendment Act of 1870 under which much of the maintenance cost of adult indoor paupers became a charge on the common poor fund. It was also helped by the activities and publicity of the Charity Organisation Society. Founded in 1869 the Organisation aimed to co-ordinate the work of private philanthropic bodies and concentrate their efforts towards the 'deserving', thereby preventing them from duplicating the activity of poor-law guardians who were seen as relieving the 'undeserving' poor. It is important to recognise that the huge funds which were at the disposal of charities could exceed those distributed by poor-law guardians. The objectives of the C.O.S. in regulating their distribution harmonised with those of the central poor law board: the last President of the Board had issued the celebrated 'Goschen Minute' in which he put forward a policy of separate spheres of influence for the poor law and charity. The spirit of the C.O.S. was also evident among guardians in thirteen unions where outdoor relief was run down and rates of pauperism declined dramatically, at least for a time. However, by the end of the nineteenth century the problem of pauperism within society seemed less alarming, because the overall rates of pauperism had declined (see figure 3). In 1834 pauperism as a percentage of population had been 8.8, whereas by 1900 it was only 2.4.

Who Pays and For Whom? Questions of Rating and Settlement

An open-ended national welfare system has bee rejected as too expensive by 1662 when, as we have seen, overseers were given power to remove applicants for relief who had no settlement in the parish. By 1834 a complex structure of common and statute law had given a number of grounds of settlement under which an individual might claim relief. Of these, the most common were parentage, birth, or in the case of women, marriage. Although the 1834 *Report* had preached a sermon on the frauds, shameful abuses, perjuries and falsehoods caused by the settlement system, and had thought only abolition would cure its evils, its actual recommendations provided for only slight modifications and these were implemented in the 1834 act. Why was such vigorous denunciation followed by such feeble reform?

In 1849 *The Times* declared that, 'The parochial system [was] the most perfect scheme ever devised between property, meritorious poverty, and idle indigence' (Roberts, 1979, p. 200). It spoke for a conservative squirearchy and clergy deeply attached to parish government and local paternalism. Passionate localism was also found in the middling classes of farmers, tradesmen and small occupiers, whose motivation sprang from a desire to keep parish rates low through personal superintendence of their nominees, the poor-law guardians. Parochial rating and settlement went hand in hand, since local ratepayers wished at most to relieve only those poor who were resident or settled in their area. The parish was therefore retained as the basis for rating and settlement in the Poor Law Amendment Act, and was not substantially modified until the 1860s.

A parochial rating system had grave defects because it assumed that there was a fairly static society with a reasonable balance between propertied and poor in each area. Since by the nineteenth century this had ceased to be the case, there was an evident tendency for the system of poor law finance to tax poverty for the relief of pauperism. Those areas with most paupers were often those with impoverished ratepayers, while wealthy localities might have few inhabitants who received relief. This created big disparities in poor rates. In industrial areas it proved difficult to tax adequately the growing commercial and industrial wealth, with the result that small householders might shoulder oppressively heavy rates. In consequence, overseers and rate-collectors were faced in depressed times with inability, or even refusal, to pay. Also, in the 'chalk and cheese' unions, as at York, where a town was linked with a substantial rural hinterland, country guardians who felt their parishes were financing a disproportionately heavy share of the rates would oppose workhouse improvements.

A fundamental irony of poor-law history was that although ratepayers' dissatisfaction with high poor rates had been a major cause of the 1834 act, the failure of the act to reform the financing of the poor law led (as we have seen) to subversion of the system by ratepayers who wished for cheaper forms of relief. The Royal Commission's *Report* of 1834 had criticised the rating system, but had failed to suggest radical reform because of the prevalent fear that a wider geographical basis for financing the poor law, through a union or national rate, would increase pauperism and poor rates. It is true that after 1834 the provision of a common fund to finance general expenditure in each union provided the basis for a gradual transition from parish to union rating. By acts of 1846, 1848 and 1861, a number of items of expenditure (including care of the sick, the lunatic, the vagrant, and the immovable poor) were charged to the common fund. The logical outcome of this process was reached in 1865 with the Union Chargeability Act which established union rating and made all relief to the poor chargeable to the common fund. A more fundamental reform had already occurred in the Irremovable Poor Act of 1861, when contributions to the common fund were changed from assessment on past levels of pauperism to the ability to pay, as estimated on the value of the property occupied. These improvements, however, did not solve the problems arising from a precarious, local system of financing the poor law. In twenty-eight Lancashire unions in 1861-5, intense distress resulting from the unemployment produced by the Cotton Famine had to be relieved from external funds produced under emergency legislation – the Union Relief Aid Act of 1862 (under which other unions in the county could be required to provide funds), and the Public Works Act of 1863 (by which loans could be obtained from the Public Works Loan Commissioners). In London, the severe winters of 1860-1 and 1866-7 led to a breakdown in poor law administration in the East End because impoverished ratepayers refused to pay for the high relief expenditures resulting from widespread unemployment. In the short term, a flood of charity from the West End bailed out the system, but by 1867 even the Poor Law Board admitted that a local poor rate had reached its limits. The pressure from the East End for an equalisation of the capital's poor rate achieved success in the

Metropolitan Poor Act of 1867 which transferred to a common fund much of the expenditure of individual unions, thus taxing the wealth of the West End for the relief of poverty in the East End.

The strong social and economic pressures which hindered a replacement of the parish as the unit of rating also perpetuated it as the basis for settlements. This was due less to a paternalist desire to relieve one's own parochial poor than to a determination to keep out the faceless poor from other parishes. This attitude was strongly held by ratepayers in close parishes, making up about one-fifth of the total, where since the late eighteenth century it had been extremely difficult for newcomers to reside, in case they gained a settlement and right to relief. Malthus, in his *Essay on the Principle of Population*, in 1789 had condemned the settlement laws as 'utterly contradictory to all ideas of freedom', and involving a 'most disgraceful and disgusting tyranny' over the poor by parish overseers. He was voicing a view common among political economists of the time in seeing these laws as an obstruction to the free labour market that economic progress required. Yet modern historians have concluded that the settlement laws before 1834 were neither as restrictive nor as expensive as contemporaries asserted.

The frequent but largely unsubstantiated complaints against the settlement laws, when accompanied by failure to reform them drastically, suggests that they may have been the scapegoat for more complex and intransigent problems. In the rural areas of the south the surplus labour problem of the early nineteenth century was not so much a product of the settlement laws caging the poor in their parish of settlement, as of population increase and agrarian depression which made employment opportunities inadequate. Implicitly the Poor Law Commission recognised this by devising a migration scheme in which, from 1835-7, redundant labourers and their families from the South of England were assisted to work in industrial areas in the North and Midlands by the efforts of two migration officers, and finance from local poor rates. A substantial proportion of the 4,323 migrants returned home again as a result both of the onset of industrial depression in 1837, which reduced employment, and of social conservatism which made it difficult for them to settle away from home. Indeed, it is arguable that the limited horizons of the rural labourer – the product of poverty and ignorance – were more notable constraints on his mobility than the settlement laws. Sometimes this problem was overcome. The poor law board ran a scheme whereby local unions could pay for poor families to find a better life in the British Colonies: it operated until 1870, and already by 1837, 6,403 people had emigrated, nearly all from the East and South-East of England.

This organised mobility was accompanied by much greater independent migration. After the creation of a national railway network in the 1840s and 1850s, there was a huge efflux from rural areas to urban, industrial ones. Local boards of guardians built up a network of reciprocal arrangements with other unions whereby each agreed to relieve, rather than remove, applicants for relief. In addition, there was extensive administering of non-resident relief, which the central poor-law board was forced to tolerate as a necessary evil: by 31 March 1846, 82,249 persons were receiving this kind of relief, which was transmitted from their parish of settlement to the parish where they resided. In this year, the Poor Removal Act conferred irremovability on those who had lived in a place for five years; in 1861 this was reduced to three, and in 1865 to one. Immunity from removal after a relatively short period of continuous residence in one place, reduced the numbers who fell foul of the laws of settlement and removal. This process was facilitated by the need for labour in the towns. Indeed, the large numbers of those receiving non-resident relief, and of those designated irremovable, suggests that the settlement laws were not a significant impediment to the creation of a free labour market.

By contrast, the rating system did impose an important constraint on the system of poor relief and on attempts to reform it. The precarious basis of local poor rates undermined the national reform of 1834. Local guardians were always conscious that they were guardians of the rates and needed to protect the interests of ratepayers. Not all of these were wealthy, as the Newcastle Guardians made clear in 1886: 'a considerable proportion of the rates are drawn from a class very little removed from pauperism, and ... any considerable increase in their burdens would have the effect of causing them to become paupers' (McCord, 1978, p. 24). At this time the resources of rural ratepayers had been squeezed by agrarian depression, and in 1896 the extent of the hardship caused was recognised by an act which relieved agricultural land of half the burden of the poor rate. Nationally, however, rateable values in the late nineteenth century were growing much faster than relief expenditures. This financial buoyancy made it possible to provide better specialist facilities within poor law institutions.

From Workhouse to Asylum, Hospital, and School

The instructions from the Royal Commission of 1832-4 to its assistant commissioners reminded them of the function of poor relief: 'It has been supposed that it was to the 43rd of Elizabeth, and to the superintendence which it forced the richer to exercise over the poorer, that we owed the industry, the orderly habits' of English labourers. In the early nineteenth century, magistrates were very active in their superintendence of rural poor relief administration; their interventions ensured a more liberal distribution of allowances than would have been given by hard-pressed ratepayers. This social paternalism was not motivated solely by benevolence but by the justices' desire to preserve order - and the existing social hierarchy - in a countryside where the discontent of unemployed labourers might otherwise turn into violence. Effectively, therefore, social paternalism and social control were fused together in the administration of the poor law. A recent study of paternalism has stated that 'the obligation to rule firmly and to guide and superintend were far more essential' to paternalism than were its accompanying benevolent duties (Roberts, 1979, p. 6). Moreover, the traditional system of social paternalism involved not only obligations by the propertied but duties by the poor: of deference, obedience, and industry. The Swing Riots of 1830 indicated that the poor were no longer fulfilling their duties, and this, it has been suggested earlier, facilitated the reforms of 1834 under which authority would be enforced more sternly through the workhouse system.

Marx described the workhouses of the New Poor Law as 'the *revenge* of the bourgeoisie upon the poor who appeal to its charity', because pauperism was seen as 'a crime to be suppressed and punished' (Meek, 1953, p. 67). While not everyone would see the issue from the same ideological standpoint, there is some evidence to suggest that the policing function of the reformed system appealed to contemporaries. In Northamptonshire unions, guardians had a strong preference for appointing former prison, army, or police officers to administer the poor law and the poor-law inspector agreed that these were just the men to detect fraudulent applications. J.G. Shaw-Lefevre, the Poor Law Commissioner, suggested that this appointments policy should not become public lest a 'dangerous cry be raised against us': however, he agreed 'that a good policeman would make a capital relieving officer' (Brundage, 1974, p. 413). Since it was these officials who were in contact with the poor, they personified the poor law as one of social control. Indeed, there was evidence in some localities of a moral policing system in which poverty was seen as a result of individual moral failure, and the greater the weakness the sterner would be the response to a request for relief. Poachers and drunkards could be denied outdoor relief, and vagrants housed in appalling casual wards, while unmarried mothers in the workhouse might be forced (illegally) to wear special uniforms to display their shame. Children in the workhouse were separated as much as possible from the moral contamination of their pauper parents, and a contemporary account described 'moral training' as pervading 'every hour of the day' (Kay and Tufnell, 1839).

The labouring poor were hostile to this system of 'moral imprisonment' and social control, and the organised Anti-Poor Law Movement of the North of England was only the more publicised part of much wider resistance. Spontaneous, intermittent and uncoordinated rural protests were also found in many areas in the rural south, as was shown by attacks on relieving officers, disturbances outside guardians' board rooms, and occasional written protests. A letter in the *Essex Standard* of 24 April 1837 was addressed to Mr. Wicked and threatened arson: 'Children from thare mothers/Men from thare waves/Starve poor families/Had better take their lives'. Overt opposition to the more stringent relief system died down, but resentment continued. Folk songs, such as the 'Song on the Times' of the 1840s, were bitterly eloquent: 'If starving, you should ask relief, you're sent to a whig bastille'. Working-class autobiographies recall vividly the anguish of entering the workhouse: Lucy Luck, a Hertfordshire strawplaiter remembered that before her mother took her into the Tring Workhouse in 1851 she stopped nearby: 'my mother sat down on the steps with one of us on each side of her, and one in her arms, crying bitterly over us before she took us into the Union' (Burnett, 1974, p. 68). Life within the Newmarket Workhouse in 1846 reminded one inmate of a gaol: 'Surrounded by walls that are too high to climb./Confined like a felon without any crime' (Longmate, 1974, p. 97).

Some contemporaries could not understand why the better material conditions within the workhouses did not attract the poor. 'The wonder is, that every labourer in the land is not eager to pauperize himself' (*Morning Chronicle,* 26 January 1850). One reason inhibiting them was that the respectable poor did not, as one of them put it, wish to be housed 'with the lawless, drinking and worthless part of the community' (Digby, 1978, p. 220). They preferred outdoor relief even if these small doles involved near-starvation and were thus 'inhumane' in their material inadequacy. Outdoor relief did not compromise respectability as did indoor relief. After 1870 there was a much greater use of indoor relief and the proportion of paupers relieved in the workhouse increased rapidly (see figures 2 and 3).

'In the workhouse there is of necessity a dead level of monotony – there are many persons but no individuals', wrote that prolific rural commentator, Richard Jeffries in 1880. By this time the herding together of the deserving and the undeserving worried thoughtful observers, who recognised the incompatibility of trying simultaneously to use the workhouse as a haven for the helpless and a deterrent for the feckless. The result was the creation of specialist agencies, which eventually discredited the concept of a general mixed workhouse. The most conspicuous group among the feckless were vagrants whose numbers increased sixfold between 1850 and 1910. Anxiety at their increasing numbers produced specialist policies to deter them: unpleasant conditions in casual wards were made even worse, while the most undeserving among the mobile poor were considered appropriate candidates for compulsory detention in labour colonies. In contrast, the deserving poor – children, the physically ill, and the aged – were given improved welfare facilities within the poor law. In addition certain categories of whom certifiable lunatics were the most numerous – received specialist treatment outside the poor law.

'One feels as though these children should be little automata instead of human beings, to obey all these clockwork arrangements' (Davenport-Hill, 1889, p. 27). This comment reveals contemporary concern about the dangers of institutionalising children within the workhouse. It led to the development in the 1870s of cottage homes (where children in large poor-law schools, such as the one at Birmingham, were divided up into much smaller groups), and in the 1890s of scattered homes (where children were dispersed into groups living with foster mothers within the community, as in Sheffield). The Sheffield pauper children attended a board school alongside the children of the independent poor, as did most workhouse children by this time. Earlier, indoor pauper children had received their schooling in individual workhouses, or occasionally, as in London, Liverpool, Manchester or Reading, in district (or 'barrack') schools that drew children from several unions. This system was dismantled unobtrusively, mainly as a result of the creation of cheap and efficient education in rate-aided board schools created after the Elementary Education Act of 1870. In the early years of the New Poor Law, workhouse schools had aimed to give pauper children 'superior eligibility' so that their better education would permit them to compete in the labour market and not become the burden on the rates which their parents had been. Some unions had a limited success in this objective, but penny-pinching by many boards of guardians, and the difficulty of recruiting efficient teachers, eroded standards to such an extent that monotonous rote-learning in the schoolroom did little either to lighten a bleak workhouse-environment or to fit a child for the world beyond it.

Children form a recognizable group within the poor law: the sick poor were harder to identify. Although cases of sickness (or alleged sickness) formed three out of every four cases of pauperism in the mid-nineteenth century, the overlapping of sickness, infirmity, and poverty was such that a harsh ideology on the relief of poverty tended to inhibit the development of more humane facilities for the sick. This was particularly evident in the early days of the New Poor Law, when there was a conspicuous lack of a coherent medical policy on the part of the central board. Parsimonious local guardians appointed medical officers at meagre salaries to supervise over-large districts, with consequent complaints from the poor of medical neglect. Efficient or energetic doctors tended to be frustrated rather than encouraged, as was shown by the efforts of Dr. Joseph Rogers to improve the treatment of sick indoor paupers in the Strand and Westminster Unions from 1856 to 1886. The needs of sick outdoor paupers (who made up two-thirds of cases of pauperism in 1870), were as much for adequate nourishment as for medicine, but doctors who precribed meat and wine as 'medical extras' tended to be regarded by guardians as usurping their monopoly over relief.

In some respects, standards of poor-law medicine gradually improved. Poor-law doctors' districts, duties and qualifications were laid down in 1842, 1847 and 1858. By the 1860s reforming pressures were strong: public opinion had been roused by the activities of newly-formed professional associations of poor-law medical officers, and by disclosures of conditions in workhouse infirmaries through the reports of the Workhouse Visiting Society after 1859 and of the 'Lancet' in 1865 and 1866. The Metropolitan Poor Act of 1867 was a response to this concern, and led the way to a better future by recognizing that the state should provide the poor with hospitals. The new asylum districts of London built hospitals or infirmaries that were quite separate from union workhouses within the district, and thus freed the sick poor from the negative policy of less eligibility. Liberated from the parsimonious attitudes of guardians, these state hospitals were able to build up very good facilities and to train nurses. Elsewhere, conditions in workhouse sick wards and infirmaries showed much less improvement. By the end of the century there was still an unfortunate dependence for nursing staff on pauper women whose capabilities were reminiscent of Sarah Gamp rather than of Agnes Jones, who had attempted to reform workhouse nursing in the way that Florence Nightingale had transformed the situation in hospitals. Two spheres of poor-law medicine which showed minimal improvement were public health and the care of the mentally ill. In both cases the preventive aspirations of social medicine were stifled by financial pressures within a destitution authority.

Moral pressures were almost as conspicuous as those of finance in the treatment by the poor law of certain categories of pauper, notably women and also the very large numbers of aged poor. The Royal Commission on the Aged Poor of 1895 found that two out of five of those over the age of 65 were paupers. For the minority among them who were inside the workhouse, treatment could vary according to their moral classification as deserving or undeserving. The deserving might merit separate or more comfortably furnished accommodation, as at Lambeth, Southwark, Bath or Norwich, or be assigned to one of the scarce rooms for aged married couples. After 1892 they might be given allowances of tobacco and snuff. For the much larger numbers of old people who received outdoor relief, the dominant concern to economise led to pitifully small doles which served only to keep the wolf from the door.

By the end of Victoria's reign, attitudes towards old people's needs were changing; considerable discussion eventually resulted in a restricted right to an old age pension in 1908. Earlier, the Medical Relief Disqualification Removal Act of 1885 had laid down that sick people receiving medical assistance from the poor law should not lose their right to vote, and hence their citizenship. Indeed, the *de facto* conversion of poor law infirmaries into state hospitals pointed the way forward to a new system of social welfare. So too did the Local Government Act of 1894 which made boards of guardians more amenable to popular pressures by widening the electorate, abolishing the property qualification for guardians, and ending *ex officio* membership. As a result there was an increase in numbers of women and of working men on the boards; they helped to humanise conditions of the sick, the old, and the young in workhouses.

The End of the Poor Law

The Royal Commission of 1832-4 had focussed on the problems of relieving rural poverty, and its reforms had been shaped by this concern. However, Victorian society was to become increasingly urbanised and industrialized: by 1901 fewer than one in four lived in a rural union compared to more than one in two in 1841, while the proportion of the population employed in agriculture had halved, from one in five to one in ten. The 1834 act assumed that the population was static and that local ratepayers should be responsible for local poverty: increasing labour mobility and the changing incidence of capital therefore created severe strains within the system during the nineteenth century.

In spite of the undoubted problems caused by changes in the social and economic structure, the framework of the New Poor Law remained intact. A very small part of local poor-law expenditure was transferred to the Exchequer, but the opportunity for radical reform, which would have occurred if a national system of taxation had been given responsibility for financing the poor law, was allowed to slip by. There was increasing interest in foreign innovations, but these were not adopted by the central poor law board. The German Social Insurance Scheme of 1883 influenced only the welfare provision that was created outside the English Poor Law. Within the poor law, policy seemed to be guided less by financial considerations than by moral ones, resulting in the reassertion of the 'principles of 1834' for the undeserving and the creation of improved facilities for the deserving. Yet by 1900 the investigations of Booth in London and Rowntree in York had emphasised the importance of economic factors – notably unemployment and low wages – rather than moral factors in causing poverty. Their discovery that nearly one-third of the population was living in poverty raised the issue of whether an old-style destitution authority, and a narrow definition of pauperism, were the appropriate bases on which to determine the welfare provisions of an advanced industrial society. In addition, concern over the problems faced by the economy in changing world markets led some people to conclude that workmen required a better welfare system if national efficiency was to be improved, and also that the relief of unemployment should be separated from the poor law. Finally, the creation of a more democratic state made a punitive workhouse system seem inappropriate as the central welfare agency within society, particularly since few paupers appeared to be able-bodied.

It was not until 1948, however, that the national system of poor relief which had begun 350 years earlier, was finally ended when the National Assistance Act stated that: 'The existing poor law shall cease to have effect'. In 1905 dissatisfaction with the poor law, and disagreement over its objectives, had led to the setting up of a Royal Commission. Its discussions had focussed on the extent to which the principles of 1834 were relevant to an urban industrial society; the appropriate demarcation between philanthropic aid and poor relief; and the relationship between the poor law and a growing number of specialist welfare agencies which were undercutting its role as a comprehensive relieving agency. The Commission had found it impossible to agree on these and other matters, and had issued Majority and Minority Reports in 1909. Both were ignored by the Liberal government, but the Local Government Board responded to them by tightening up its administration, especially on indoor relief. Over the next three decades the poor law was gradually dismantled. The workhouse was rechristened a poor law institution in 1913. Indoor relief was increasingly confined to the 'helpless poor' – children, old people and the sick. Under the Local Government Act of 1929 local authorities were encouraged to take over these poor-law institutions as hospitals. The same act ended the use of the term 'pauper'. It also abolished the boards of guardians; but the Public Assistance Committees which replaced them handed out means-tested benefits which some of the poor regarded as almost as oppressive as the old outdoor relief. Parallel to this process of attrition an alternative welfare system developed along quite different principles. The National Insurance Act of 1911 began the provision of social insurance, which was gradually extended to a growing proportion of the working population until it became universal in 1946. This principle of compulsory contribution for benefits received as of right was central to the momentous reforms of 1945-8 which established the modern welfare state. The Foreign Secretary, Ernest Bevin, celebrated the passing of the National Assistance Act of 1948 with the words 'At last we have buried the poor law'.

Select Bibliography

Ashforth, D., 'The Urban Poor Law' in D. Fraser (ed), *The New Poor Law in the Nineteenth Century* (1976)

Baugh, D.A., 'The Cost of Poor Relief in South-East England', *Ec. Hist. Rev.* (second series, XXVIII, 1975)

Blaug, M., 'The Myth of the Old Poor Law and the Making of the New', *J. Ec. Hist.* (XXIII, 1963)

Blaug, M., 'The Poor Law Report Re-examined', *J. Ec. Hist.* (XXIV, 1964)

Boyson, R., 'The New Poor Law in North-East Lancashire 1834-71', *Trans. of the Lancs. & Cheshire Antiq. Soc.* (LXX, 1960)

Brundage, A., 'The English Poor Law and the Cohesion of Agricultural Society', *Agricultural History* (XLVIII, 1974)

Brundage, A., *The Making of the New Poor Law. The politics of inquiry, enactment and implementation, 1832-39* (1978)

Burnett, J. (ed), *Useful Toil: Autobiographies of working people from the 1820s to the 1920s* (1974)

Cowherd, R.G., *Political Economists and the English Poor Laws. A Historical Study of the Influence of Classical Economics on the Formation of Social Welfare Policy* (1977)

Crowther, M.A., 'The Later Years of the Workhouse 1890-1929' in P. Thane (ed), *The Origins of British Social Policy* (1978)

Davenport-Hill, F., *Children of the State* (1889)

Dickens, A., 'The Architect and the Workhouse', *Architectural Review* (160, 1976)

Digby, A., 'The Labour Market and the Continuity of Social Policy after 1834: the Case of the Eastern Counties', *Ec. Hist. Rev.* (second series, XXVIII, 1975)

Digby, A., 'The Rural Poor Law' in D. Fraser (ed), *The New Poor Law in the Nineteenth Century* (1976)

Digby, A., *Pauper Palaces* (1978)

Digby, A., 'The Relief of Poverty in Victorian York: Attitudes and Policies' in C.H. Feinstein (ed), *York 1831-1981* (1981)

Digby, A., 'The Rural Poor' in G.E. Mingay (ed), *The Victorian Countryside* (2 vols, 1981)

Duke, F., 'Pauper Education' in D. Fraser (ed), *The New Poor Law in the Nineteenth Century* (1976)

Dunkley, P., 'The "Hungry Forties" and the New Poor Law: A Case Study', *Hist. J.* (XVII, 1974)

Dunkley, P., 'Paternalism, the Magistracy and Poor Relief in England', *International Rev. of Soc. Hist.* (XXIV, 1979)

Edsall, N.C., *The anti-Poor Law movement* (1971)

Flinn, M.W., 'Medical Services under the New Poor Law' in D.
Fraser (ed), *The New Poor Law in the Nineteenth Century* (1976)

Fraser, D. (ed), *The New Poor Law in the Nineteenth Century* (1976)

Hampson, E.M., *The Treatment of Poverty in Cambridgeshire* (1934)

Henriques, U.R.Q., 'How Cruel was the Victorian Poor Law?',
Hist. J. (XI, 1968)

Hobsbawm, E.J. and Rudé, G., *Captain Swing* (1969)

Holderness, B.A., '"Open" and "Close" Parishes in England in
the Eighteenth and Nineteenth Centuries', *Ag. Hist. Rev.* (20, 1972)

Huzel,J.P., 'The Demographic Impact of the Old Poor Law', *Ec.
Hist. Rev.* (second series, XXXIII, 1980)

Jefferies, R., *Hodge and His Masters* (2 vols, 1880)

Kay, J.P. and Tufnell, E.C., *Reports on the Training of Pauper
Children* (1839)

Longmate, N., *The Workhouse* (1974)

Lubenow, W.C., *The Politics of Government Growth* (1971)

McCloskey, D., 'New Perspectives on the Old Poor Law', *Explorations
in Ec. Hist.* (X, 1973)

McCord, N., 'The Implementation of the 1834 Poor Law Amendment
Act on Tyneside', *Int. Rev. Soc. Hist.* (XIV, 1969)

McCord, N., 'The Poor Law and Philanthropy' in D. Fraser (ed),
The New Poor Law in the Nineteenth Century (1976)

McCord, N., 'Ratepayers and Social Policy' in P. Thane (ed),
The Origins of British Social Policy (1978)

Meek, R.L. (ed), *Marx and Engels on Malthus* (1953)

Midwinter, E.C., *Social Administration in Lancashire 1830-1860*
(1969)

Mills, D.R., *Lord and Peasant in Nineteenth-Century Britain* (1980)

Neuman, M., 'Speenhamland in Berkshire' in E.W. Martin (ed),
Comparative Development in Social Welfare (1972)

Oxley, G.W., *Poor Relief in England and Wales 1601-1834* (1974)

Palmer, R (ed), *A Touch on the Times. Songs of Social Change
1770-1914* (1974)

Pember Reeves, M., *Round About A Pound A Week* (1979 edition)

Poynter, J.R., *Society and Pauperism. English Ideas on Poor
Relief, 1795-1834* (1969)

Redford, A., *Labour Migration in England, 1800-1850* (second
edition, 1964)

Roberts, D., *Victorian Origins of the Welfare State* (1960)

Roberts, D., 'How Cruel was the Victorian Poor Law?',
Historical Journal (VI, 1963)

Roberts, D., *Paternalism in Early Victorian England* (1979)

Rose, M.E., 'The Allowance System under the New Poor Law',
Ec. Hist. Rev. (second series, XIX, 1966)

Rose, M.E., 'The New Poor Law in an Industrial Area' in R.M.
Marshall (ed), *The Industrial Revolution* (1970)

Rose, M.E., 'The Anti-Poor Law Agitation' in J.T. Ward (ed),
Popular Movements c1830-50 (1970)

Rose, M.E. (ed), *The English Poor Law 1780-1930* (1971)

Rose, M.E. 'Settlement, Removal and the New Poor Law' in D. Fraser
  (ed), *The New Poor Law in the Nineteenth Century* (1976)
Searby, P., 'The Relief of the Poor in Coventry, 1830-60',
  Hist. J. (XX, 1977)
Stedman Jones, G., *Outcast London* (1976)
Taylor, J.S., 'The Unreformed Workhouse, 1776-1834' in E.W.
  Martin (ed), *Comparative Development in Social Welfare* (1972)
Taylor, J.S., 'The Impact of Pauper Settlement 1691-1834',
  Past and Present (73, 1976)
Thane, P., 'Women and the Poor Law in Victorian and Edwardian
  England', *History Workshop Journal* (6, 1978)
Thomas, E.G., 'The Old Poor Law and Medicine', *Med. Hist.*
  (24, 1980)
Thompson, E.P., 'The Moral Economy of the English Crowd in
  the Eighteenth Century', *Past and Present* (50, 1971)
Vorspan, R., 'Vagrancy and the New Poor Law in Late-Victorian
  and Edwardian England', *Eng. Hist. Rev.* (XCII, 1977)
W.E.A. Eastern District, *In and Out of the Workhouse. The
  Coming of the New Poor Law to Cambridgeshire and
  Huntingdonshire* (1978)
Webb, S and B., *English Poor Law History* (parts 1 and 2,
  3 vols, 1963 edition)